Full Blood

JOHN SIDDIQUE was born in 1964. His discovery of his local library when young began his life-long love affair with what words mean and how they sit together. He is the bestselling author of *Recital—An Almanac*, *Poems From A Northern Soul*, *The Prize* and now *Full Blood*. He is the co-author of the story/memoir *Four Fathers*.

He has contributed poems, stories, essays and articles to many publications, including *Granta*, *The Guardian*, *Poetry Review*, and *The Rialto*.

The Prize, published to wide acclaim in 2005, was nominated for the Forward Prize. His children's book *Don't Wear It On Your Head* was shortlisted for the CLPE Poetry Award in 2007. On publication in 2009, *Recital* was described as "one of the most important British poetry books of the last twenty years" by Lauri Ramey of CSULA. Jackie Kay describes Siddique's writing as "a brilliant balancing act."

Siddique is admired for his captivating readings and his infectious love of literature. He teaches poetry and creative writing in the UK and abroad, and has worked with The British Council, The Arvon Foundation, The Poetry School and The Poetry Society. He has a website at www.johnsiddique.co.uk

Also by John Siddique

POETRY
  The Prize (The Rialto, 2005)
  Poems from a Northern Soul (Crocus, 2007)
  Recital—An Almanac (Salt, 2009)

PROSE
  Four Fathers with Ray French, James Nash and Tom Palmer
    (Route, 2006)

FOR CHILDREN
  Don't Wear It On Your Head, Don't Stick It Down Your Pants (Salt,
    2010)

AS EDITOR
  Transparency (Crocus, 2005)

Full Blood

John Siddique

SALT

LONDON

PUBLISHED BY SALT PUBLISHING
Acre House, 11–15 William Road, London NW1 3ER, United Kingdom

Salt Publishing 2011
Reprinted with corrections 2011

Printed and bound in the United Kingdom by Lightning Source UK Ltd

Typeset in Swift 9.5 / 13

ISBN 978 1 84471 824 5 paperback

1 3 5 7 9 8 6 4 2

for Abha

'*Write beautifully what people don't want to hear*'
— FREDERICK SEIDEL

Contents

Acknowledgements

Poems in this work were originally published in the following publications:

MAGAZINES
'Every Atom', 'For Our Final Fuck Of The Afternoon'—*Poetry Review*
'A Place Of Silence', 'Love Poem'—*The Rialto*
'Coffee Mornings'—*The Literary Review*
'Jali', 'Kitying', 'Abha', 'Junmo', 'Maria'—*Moving Worlds Journal*
'Kabul'—*Nthposition*
'The Learning Skin'—*Gargoyle*
'Sunday'—*The North*

ANTHOLOGIES
'Name', 'Adultery', 'Afghanistan 1970'—*The Harper Collins Anthology of English Poetry by Indians*
'Rain Song'—*Soul Feathers: Anthology for MacMillan Cancer Support* (Indigo Dreams)
'Green Dogs'—*Pendulum: The Poetry of Dreams* (Avalanche Books)

A list of further acknowledgements can be found at the end of this collection.

Prologue

Every Atom

'For every atom belonging to me as good as belongs to you'
— WALT WHITMAN

Each of us changes when placed next to the other.
We place ourselves, or are placed or paired creating
stories, a new idea, sometimes love.

With love comes the desire to be seen for who we are.
From juxtaposition comes the marriage of existence.
Arranging ourselves as an exhibition of human things.

Marriages of the married and unmarried,
so many bedrooms and doorways.
Arranging ourselves as an exhibition of human things.

The marriage of shadow and light,
born to an impermanent sun.

The music between the strings, between the staves,
between the musician and the notes.

The sea and the sky unified at one horizon.

Body, mind—action and consequence.

The writer and his notebook learning
the sacrament of ink.

The dancer and gravity illustrate the music
of freedom and force.

The portrait given soul by the painter
going beyond technique.

Wedding rings on hands held together and apart.

Arranging ourselves:
As gold and steel.
As youth and old age.
As prayer and its church.
As Christ in the garden.
As cobalt is to the truth of the sky.
As the sound of the Om.
As Omega.
As Alpha, and what comes before and after
              —the seed of the sound.
An exhibition of human things.
A cup turned by hand, held by other hands.
The immigrant wedding in colours
you didn't even know you could wish for.
Seagrass and sand dune, roots and mass
              —they are entwined.
Wave and ocean
              —water given life from her movement,
                          from his depth.

The exhibition of human things.
A country and its people / The statistics and the individual.
No country without the individual, no marriage without
each partner existing within themselves.

No marriage without one being seen by the other.
No marriage without the creation of context.
Consider the decisions, the fragments we make.
Alpha—love used as a verb. Omega—love as a choice.

Love sometimes is not a choice—it is just is, or is not.
I place my life here and it means something if I choose it to.
We place our lives together and they mean something
if we choose them to.

We tell our stories for there are always stories.
The dancer knows how earth and body relate.
The poet journeys the pen through the connections.

We choose to believe in statistics or the mystery.
The mystery of marriage—between each thing,
Between the life of each moment—the mystery of marriage
—the mystery of human things.

Via Negativa

A whistle in the dark is still a whistle
— GIDEON LEVY

Thirst

Imagine thirst without knowing water.
And you ask me what freedom means.
Imagine love without love.

Some things are unthinkable,
until one day the unthinkable is here.
Imagine thirst without knowing water.

Some things we assume just are as they are,
no action is taken to make or sustain them.
Imagine love without love.

It is fear that eats the heart: fear and
endless talk, and not risking a step.
Imagine thirst without knowing water.

Fold away your beautiful thoughts.
Talk away curiosity, chatter away truth.
Imagine love without love.

Imagine believing in the whispers,
the screams and the gossip. Dancing to a tune
with no song to sing inside you.
Imagine love without love.

The Knife

1. THE NATIONAL FRONT

Their mouths full of fire and alcohol;
they patrol the town; night and weekends.
Two main no-go zones—the bus station,
and the shopping centre—out of town it's not
good to go through Littleborough or Whitworth.

Their faces contort with boiling spit,
holding the fire narrows their eyes.
Everyone wears a uniform,
rockers are rockers, ska kids—mods,
the NF—skinheads; shaven heads, shirts
buttoned right up, drainpipe trews, everything
tight. The eighteen holes of oxblood red
Dr. Martin boots, the green of flight jackets.

These are the rules—Never be in the bus station
or the market at night, not even if
you are with friends. Always stick to the main streets
but have a side street escape route planned.
Make sure you are carrying a knife.
Learn the art of invisibility. Remember
that you continually run the gauntlet.

Their eyes are cold in the heat of their heads,
predators. It is no use holding your head high,
or fighting back in defiance—you will die,
it is a matter of will, antagonism and terror.
They have the mentality—you do not.
Read your books, go from house to house, live
within sanctuaries, the streets are theirs.
It has been this way for twenty years,
some of the gangs are fathers and sons,
at home they must smile at their children
and wives and speak words of longing and love.

Tattooed pride, white power, a moon swastika,
Rochdale F.C. the football ground is a Mecca
every other Saturday afternoon
for home games. On these days we go into town,
try to chat up girls, gather and talk
in front of W.H. Smith's for a few hours.
Whilst they cry with pride, curse the other team
and gang fight. *'Up the Dale, Down the ale.'*
A fourth division football team supported
by first division hardcore—The Cocks of The North.

Their fire is fuelled with alcohol, their fire
is fuelled with spit, their fire burns in cold eyes,
their fire is wet as napalm on the lips.
Their fire is a steel hard mind. The first pulses
deep in the balls, in the pit of the stomach,
a moment of orgasm, it lights in fists and feet
and slogans, the clean white beauty of violence.

2. ANDREA OR JULIE

Andrea on my left,
I am full of desire,
or was it Julie I
was walking to the bus,
both of them are written
in my inner pathways,
but time switches people
around when you try to
think of them.

3. ANDREA

I never went out with Andrea,
I got her number when I overheard
her saying it aloud on the way home
one day, burned it into my mind,
mantric repetition. Took my life
in my hands in the close cell of a public
call box that night to speak to her.

Frothy coffee in little glass cups at
melamine tables in brown leatherette
booths, talking about rock music, and bands,
no kisses, not holding hands, only wishes
—then I would curse my brown skin, curse
my impossible name. I don't know
why we used to meet, she seemed ageless,
dark tumbling, a window I wanted
to see through.

Dear Andrea,
though I can't even remember what you
look like, the lightning spark
is still written there.

4. ROCHDALE BUS STATION

It was modern then, the black glass
of the council office tower,
silver steps of escalators
feeding you in and out, orange
rubber floor tiles (hospital clean)
paving the way to each bus stand.

Two corridors of departure
and arrival centred around
the architectural cement
of the bus lanes. You could go all
over on the Greater Manchester buses,
and we did, to parties in Halifax,
the oxbow river at Daisy Nook
for walks and hanging out, Royton Park,
Manchester city centre.

At night when the frequency of
travellers dies down, the buses only
run every hour or so, there is a lot
of waiting to be done. Andrea and I
have forty minutes to wait,
she gets the 452 towards Littleborough.
Looking out to the lit up face
of the town hall clock, the town taxi rank
across the way, we talk as teenagers
talk, this song, that teacher.

See you she says as I unrequitedly watch
her climb onto the bus. Her loose dark
curls, the paleness of her skin, her lovely
hand as she pulls herself up the step,
holding the shining pole by the bus doors.
I go hot inside, an erection betrays

me in my 501s, but she has taken her seat.
I wait some more for her bus to pull away,
she glances a bit and gives a simple wave
as she sets off. I walk out the long way
through the stands to Milton Street,
the climb of the steep hill of John Street.

5. JOHN STREET

There was no one behind me when I left
the bus station. A warm September night,
drawn with lights from Lennon's supermarket
at the top of the hill, the overgrown garden
of St. James' Church lies ahead with its secrets.
I know they are behind me. I can feel them
in the deeper layers of my skin, I am for it
if I try to run. A laugh, a response,
paki bastard said low, two or three of them.

They are faster than me, they are gaining,
trying to look bigger, taller, maybe I can
run once I hit the corner near the church.
Twenty yards, three of them. The enough
in me moves my hand to my pocket,
perhaps if they see the knife they'll think again.
Flick and it is open, the orange reflection
of street lamps on its blade. I put the open
knife into my pocket, shift my hand
to my best grip, they are around me.

It begins with a question, *have you got the time?*
No breath, I am hot water, scorched mouth.
They are in full regalia, red boots and green jackets,
shaven heads make them look animal.
The main one speaks, the others go to back up mode,
You paki cunt, his Adam's apple bobbles,
a bubble of spit on his bottom lip,
I know you have a knife, I'll take it off you
and shove it up your arse. He's as skinny as fuck,
wiry, a gold earring in his left ear.
The other two are shadow at the edge

of wet fear. I am small and dirty in my skin,
expecting a fist to my head. *Cunt*
—a breath of beer. *If I see you you're dead.*
They walk off laughing in the direction
I want to go in, I am static amongst
the tufts of grass that have grown on soil,
that was turned too long ago, left littered
with half bricks and steel mesh.

Love Poem

She works from seven in the morning
until late at night, her main job
and other jobs squeezed in,
not leaving a moment
to notice the sleeping animal of her body,
how it cannot wake up to open its claws,
press its pads to the ground, pull its spine
in both directions forcing the curve down
through her belly.

She avoids loneliness,
        keeping her animal body
                unconscious.

        Ears twitch back
in the few moments of REM sleep
—a tiger under streetlights
on an empty boulevard;
unlit stores, a police siren far away.

Memorial Day

Sunday late Spring sun ascends
over section 60 of Arlington Cemetery,
as girl scouts plant small plastic flags
on the rows of graves.

Music of bugles, silence of prayers
learned especially for today.
Drums strike the air,
a beautiful warm day across these States.

Sections 1 through 60; there could be
generations of families here,
great-great-grandfather down to only son,
perhaps a daughter now.

The sun ascends to fall over the years
which march forward in dignified rows,
war by war, and white stone by white stone,
peace by peace, ending by ending.

Mary

Screaming woman at Venice beach, yesterday
she was yelling at the big cars. She had yelled
for so long there were no more words, only
the broken-throated caw cry of crow.

She traverses Washington Boulevard marking
out her territory from Via Marina
to the Pacific itself. Standing on
the cement pier among the fishing poles,
making tai chi movements with her arms.

Her skin is healthy, rude and reddened by
daily sun, freshened by the ocean breeze.
Her nails are clean; her corduroy coat is tidy.

The punters flinch when she sits down outside
a café. *My name is Mary. Just let me explain.*

One Monday Afternoon in Mytholmroyd

You can't see what is down the road from behind
the wheel in a line of traffic. There are always
roadworks up ahead on this single road to take you
through the hills of the Calder Valley. One road in,

one road out is what they say around here.
The horns begin tooting like the rising expectation
of a football match—punctuated by shouts
between blasts, yells of ecstasy or fury.

Twenty minutes and no movement, a crowd
has left their cars and are clustered around
a small silver one—someone has died at the wheel
and everyone has cursed them for holding them up
on the journey home, shame and guilt upon us.

But no one has died, I walk the line of cars
expecting to see someone trying to give kisses of life.
We stand silent, there is a blonde woman
at the wheel, the car's hazards blinking seconds,
she is in her late forties, she looks tired,
her hair is too brassy, she has simply
come to a stop on this road.

No movement, no indication of anything
in her face. She could be a mannequin placed
in a car as a practical joke—we don't know what to do,
no use banging her window or shouting.

Rachel Last Springtime

She leans in to put her arms around him as if
she is a child hanging onto her daddy's neck.
She wants love, she leans in. He sits straight
as she leans, he is still and doesn't speak,
well he speaks, but he doesn't say anything.
He said once, *I've never missed anything*
or anyone in my life. She holds on, leans in,
extracting the idea of love from her own
wanting to be loved, making familiarity
and sex into something they're not, as if
the reflection of the thing was the thing itself.
They stay up late, she watches the couple
they make in the dining room window.
He plays music files on the computer,
this is a good one, he says. The wall lights
cast a pale white that puts a shadow between
them, she leans into this to kiss him, tells him
she loves him, fishing for his depths.

Coffee Mornings

This town has perished at occasional tables,
where we meet occasionally for coffee,
and the names we lash perish in our unsewing circle.

Occasionally one tries to break free,
to run out of the valley, it's a long road
scattered with the greying bones of those
without enough escape velocity.
Those who have perished serve as a warning
to all who would try.

There is the occasional dissent at the table.
There are the occasional objections
to our power, at these times we use absolute force:
the undermine through gossip, the slap down,
the revealing of intimate details
that never quite happened the way they are being
told. The perished walk around—hungry ghosts
of shoppers, finding little succour in the Co-op
between the bread and the beer aisles.

The Learning Skin

She pisses herself as she feels she is falling.
Thinks of white goods as the stone wave breaks.
Things in the fridge. The washing-up not done.
Her belly full of air-sick fire,

it is safer

lying down. There are some with little dust
in their eyes. There are those whose eyes are covered
in mud. All in the skin, her sense of moment.

All the extra torn down. Loose change in her pocket.
She waits for a letter. She unbreaks her soul
in the bindweed, and the feel of the turned soil
at her feet. Every morning outside she is deaf
to the roar, senses turned in where everyone

pulls at her.

She breaks feeding the birds. Each small movement
a reminder of the last trip they made.
Just running. Arms in.

Under the light. Under the wisdom of diamonds.
Under the unlearned impossible news,
the toast browns. She never buys snack food
so she eats a lot of bread. Keeping the stereo low.
Her extra self rises out, leaving her to light the incense.
To watch the shade change as the day comes on.

Touches her hip and her hair. *This is me
washed, rinsed through.* Too many gods call her
—come to sleep now.

Her stomach bloats a little with the toast.
In the sickness she lies down on her bed.
The birds sound like burglars. It all comes in
through her skin. Her own weight against cotton.

Her hips and hair.

The Last Poem

I remember you on the curving
escalators of Charles de Gaulle airport.

Fifty yards apart. Taking turns to photograph
each other in the belly of this space station.

I didn't know then that we were trying
to discern each other. Each photo flawed proof,
pictures of things that don't really have names,
though this future makes us count and name
those fragments, matching numbers, rechecking
the facts, fixing these images of us.

I want to turn and say look, look here, it was real.

The silver walkway feeding travellers in,
moving us out into our adventures,
all that machinery; cables and cogs
under metal. Your turn, then my turn,
catching the moment to prove the love.

Kabul

The Kabul cuts its angles while boys arch
their spines, talk and swim, hanging their feet
over the river walls. Cooling the sun and the dust
from their backs, soaking their shirts to stay fresh.

The brown walls of every building, the colour
of the mud, skitter arabesques. If I took a pen
to your maps, I could find every shape.
Black ink puzzling out swastikas for the sun
and moon. Every corner a curve in the name of god.

Camels camp next to apartment blocks.
Volkswagen Beetles dry chugging to cool
their engines. A Pashtun boy with the face
of a goddess, eyes lined with kohl, and a smile
for the eye of the heart. Bright carpets air
on the river wall. Small birds in cages
sing in the barbershop over men's talk.
Next door a Mongol child in red woollens,
red jacket, repairs shoes on an anvil
with tacks, and a hammer bigger than his hand.

Chickens are for sale. Mountain men
with their beards of stone come away
with their purchases. If beards could talk
there would be some stories. This is before
Russia, the Taliban or America close the books,
making fires of knowledge and truths.

A wedding party, pink, red and green
on top of a minibus, beating a drum.

Our orange 'Seddon Diesel' heads out of the city
onto the mountain road. We hold on tight,
to this sheer pathway with tumbling death

on each side. Into the snow with hot hearts
from the streets, heat and dust.
Between here and the pass our only company
are the goats finding something to live on.
We stop for a while to look back. I'm five years old.
Afghanistan kisses the eyes of my heart.

One Hundred

Christopher John Reed.
Travis Mackin.
Tom Sawyer.
Danny Winter.
Richard Robinson.
Daniel Nield.
Darren Smith.
Stephen Kingscott.
Jamie Gunn.
Paul Upton.
I have never seen
skies so blue.

Tom Gaden.
Michael Laski.
Christopher Harkett.
Graeme Stiff.
Dean John.
Tobie Fasfous.
Sean Binnie.
Adrian Sheldon.
Ben Ross.
Kumar Pun.
Sky catches its breath
on the mountaintops.

Jason Mackie.
Petero Suesue.
Jordan Rossi.
Martin Richards.
Kieron Hill.
Stephen Bolger.
Nigel Moffett.
Cyrus Thatcher.

Robert McLaren.
Skies so blue
you could fall into them.

Paul Mervis.
Sean Birchall.
Rupert Thorneloe.
Joshua Hammond.
David Dennis.
Robert Laws.
Dane Elson.
Ben Babington-Browne.
Christopher Whiteside.
Daniel Hume.
Clear river, bluest sky.

John Brackpool.
Lee Scott.
Daniel Simpson.
Joseph Murphy.
James Backhouse.
William Aldridge.
Jonathan Horne.
Aminiasi Toge.
Joseph Etchells.
Daniel Shepherd.
Panjshir Valley as green
as England in the rains.

Christopher King.
Craig Hopson.
Sean Upton.
Phillip Lawrence.
Anthony Lombardi.
Kyle Adams.

Kevin Mulligan.
Dale Hopkins.
Jason Williams.
Daniel Wild.
Desert mouthed mountains
take our breath.

Matthew Hatton.
Mark Hale.
Richard Hunt.
Simon Valentine.
Louis Carter.
Simon Annis.
James Fullarton.
Johnathon Young.
Paul McAleese.
Shaun Bush.
The boiling spray
of the Helmand river.

Lee Houltram
Kevin Elliott.
Stuart Millar.
Richard Brandon.
Gavin Elliott.
John Harrison.
Jason Dunn-Bridgeman.
Brett Hall.
Stuart McGrath.
Michael Lockett.
Fields of waist high poppies.

James Prosser.
Marcin Wojtak.
Jamie Janes.

James Hill.
James Oakland.
Thomas Mason.
Olaf Schmid.
Nicholas Webster-Smith.
Steven Boote.
Jimmy Major.
Petals as light as butterfly wings.

Matthew Telford.
Darren Chant.
Phillip Scott.
Philip Allen.
Samuel Bassett.
Andrew Fentiman.
Loren Marlton-Thomas.
Robert Loughran-Dickson.
John Amer.
Adam Drane.
I have never seen
skies so blue.

One Hundred

Saifullah.
KoKo Gul.
Zarifi.
Amin.
Arbabrahim.
Sadar Wali.
Muhammad Wali.
Umar Khan.
Sher Ali Aqa.
Abadullah.
I have never seen
skies so blue.

Mutahar.
Saadullah.
Ajab.
Zrawar.
Sher Afzal.
Amanullah.
Habibullah.
Esmatullah Zia.
Palwasha.
Safaida.
Hearts of the green valleys.

Jawed Norzahie.
Ali Nazar.
Par Mina.
Jamila.
Mariam.
Asarajah.
Gul Khobana.
Hawa.
Bas Maro.

Bakht Mina.
Wedding voices
ring the mountain walls.

Taj Maro.
Hayat Bibi.
Bakht Mina.
Gul Bibi.
Shughia.
Gul Wona.
Nazanin.
Lal Maro.
Ahsanulla.
Karimullah.
Homes made from
the mud of the Earth.

Habib.
Sharifa.
Atifa.
Khan Mohammad.
Shirin.
Namro.
Farida.
Abdullah.
Shazia.
Fatima.
Hussun Pari.
River meets the desert.

Sater Bibi.
Brishna.
Hijrana.
Zarlashta.
Hukum Khan.

Gul Maro.
Abdullah.
Aziza.
Wahida.
Gulab Zari.
The poppies and the trees.

Zeba.
Tahira.
Nazia.
Shekiba.
Shir Bano.
Gul Dasta.
Atifa.
Shahnaz.
Badam Hanif.
Marjan.
Mazes of low walls
lead eyes to blue

Haji Sardar.
Shekh Anwar.
Sheri Ali.
Norullah.
Noral.
Torgul Mohammad Masom.
Feda Mohammad.
Abdullah Khan.
Haji Dastangul.
Basgul Dastangul.
Zig-Zag lines write lives.

Mohammada Gul.
Sayeda Gul.
Denar Gul.
Amir Painda.
Haji Abdul Qadoos.
Abdul Rauf.
Qabol Khan.
Abdul Khaliq.
Abdul Rashid.
Abdul Shakir.
The iron of the beard.

Abdul Nasir.
Abdul Qadir.
Abdul Latif.
Nadia Khan.
Aimal Khan.
Safia Khan.
Zia-ul-Haq.
Malem Mohammad Nader.
Mohammad Musa Khan.
Behnooshahr.
The blue eye of the desert.

*Note that where a surname has not been given
I have appended the family name where possible.*

Afghanistan 1970, Stopped

We're somewhere
in Afghanistan. The five-year-old in me
can't remember the town's name.
Our minibus up high
on a police transporter, for our own protection.

The hill bandits
are raiding, kidnapping at random.
We don't know the roads.
We're stopped for the night. Father climbs down
the lorry, finds seehk kebabs
from somewhere. They are hot and flecked
with green chilli.
An illicit midnight picnic in a country
that's closed for takeaway.

The shutters are down.
There is no news on the news.
Night, dust and heat still in my mouth.

Filey

The toilet block down from
the chalets, I'm standing next
to my father at the urinal.
He has a three-week beard hiding
his mouth. The black Ford Zodiac
is parked on the grass in front of
our accommodation.

Brown tile, a large spider
in the sink, disinfectant
cubes in the piss tray.

My father is next to me,
it is eight in the morning.
Forty years ago. It is late summer.

My mother and sister are making
breakfast, dad and I have set out
together to wash, and he's telling
me about the sea and the coast
and how sand gets everywhere.

Blue

The secret of the bluest sky
is that there is no colour above,
that if you fell into it, you would never stop.
Thank gravity for holding you up
on the ceiling of the ground. The temptation
to fall into the perfect blue
as if she was water, and beneath
her still surface an infinite black.

I Think of You

This year I reclaimed the 'Spring Wood'.
I haven't walked there since it was ours.
It's the same place, the huge rocks placed
down by glaciers before we knew anything.

We're as temporary as the bluebells
that come up in springtime, we shall be
wild garlic memories before we know it.

I think of you, though we may not speak,
though I go out of my way not to see you.
I think of you in a before it all happened way.

I love the bluebells growing in the green,
the permanence that each rock assures us of,
I think of you,
the green of the wood,
the bluebells and the stones.

Parenthesis

I tore my mother on the way out.
All night of the twenty fourth of July
she laboured, I arrived at nine a.m.

They put me to one side as they stitched her,
those first moments; I belonged to myself.
I knew who I was right then, the light
of the womb, the light of conscious spark,
the light of being and ether. My eyes saw little,
they did not work clearly yet. I was full
and I was empty, wrapped in a white blanket,
in a clear plastic cot, the vagueness of
curtains, a large face looking over me
from time to time, the rumble of my father's
voice shivering in my chromosomes.

I knew my name, which I have now forgotten.
I had made a list, or the list had made me,
there was a single word amongst the suddenness
of experience, of what comes before
you and after you — continuity.

Blackbird, Silence Your Shrill Song

Tortured soul today, a shrill song crying for water
in the bitter cold of the first winter.

I worry for you hanging around the street every day.
I don't know what you want. I worry for you,
for the cat's teeth and claws you could meet,
for the heartache you put into me with your harsh voice.

Blackbird at New Year sing your other song,
to open the portal to the other place,
connection and meaning, where the ordinary is
totemic, where the truth of symbols ripple away
into love, community and honour.

Shrill song opening the gate to purgatory,
trapping the damned until judgement. We have
all been so greedy and self-concerned
these last thirty years, afraid of each other,
fixing our mask faces over our truth.

I know that you have come to take us to an
in-between place. The cats stay away from you.

Listen, listen don't take us yet, wait a while
in the bare cherry tree. We are learning
the hard way about the hollowness of the heart,
that we have tried to buy life only to end up
with addictions to images and machines.

Silence your shrill song—guard us now. Watch over
us from your perch, we have heard your warning.

My Beautiful Fantasist

I have closed my eyes against you,
removed you from my blood.
I cast you out.

You were the iron that reddened
my waters, the magnet of my polarisation.
I have closed my eyes against you.

With the ritual of seeing you again,
after your story of love had faded.
I cast you out.

After your passion turned out to be an escape.
After you had met another.
I have closed my eyes against you.

The heat we generated,
all we would ever do is burn.
I cast you out.

With the ritual of my worst behaviours,
with self-talk, with pigeon chest.
With bastard words said lovingly
—I cast you out

Pig

Blushing heat through course hair, my hand upon
his back. He throws himself down with a sigh.
A broken-hearted pig in a field by
the February river. Moss glows in
the cold damp air, clinging on to the north
face of dry stone walling. Pig is completely
still, only his stomach lifting with his breath.
Neither of us can move — my heart to his
heart, secured by a tie forever now.
He cries a little. Little black eyes, girlish
eyelashes. Tomorrow I'll bring him peelings,
not think of the day when his field is empty.

There Were Birds

What I miss the most these days are the birds.
I was sitting at my window the day
the birds stopped singing,
I wondered who else had heard them stop.

There was nothing on the news, the day the birds
stopped singing. There were stories showing:
greed, hatred and delusion, but nothing
about birds, or how the sky was not alive anymore.

They all stopped at the same time,
it came on the news eventually.
I went to the woods, the birds had all fallen
to the ground, the day the birds stopped singing.

If I tried to describe a bird to you now
—you who have been born in the time after
the birds stopped singing, I would move my hands
as if they were a fantasy; the sky is not alive.

If I told you stories from the before-time,
whistled their songs, you would frown and perhaps
smile at the impossibility of my fictions,
of the day that the birds stopped singing.

True Roses of England

After D.H. Lawrence

Where are the true roses of England?
Those who freely offer their faces
to the air in all complexity. Offering
their scent
                    —the essence of sun, rain and soil.

True roses of England, making the garden
alive with presence. Not just a pretty
decoration or some undisciplined thing.

The courage of the true rose to gift its beauty;
such Godly wildness contained in your flowering.
Daring to give yourself fully in a world,
where sentiment has overtaken feeling.
Beware the shallows of thornless years.
Offer your openness with no thought of loss.

Reclaiming the Body

You only live twice:
Once when you're born
And once when you look death in the face
— IAN FLEMING

Name

Put your hands on me to remind me who
I am, put your hands on my face and heart
and say my name to stop me still, make me
human, teach me to wait until I can open
with self-blessing, as a rose buds to the sun,
as a seal on a rock sings the sea.

All it would take is a word, and day
and night would separate, the oceans would
move back to reveal the land, until one day
a figure would emerge from the tall grasses,
he would look out from his own two eyes
—the seed heads ripening, the wind causing
them to hush, the hills in the distance,
he would stand in the newly made
and know his own name again.

Between the Words

You won't risk your heart in my company.
I shutter my heart beneath the breastbone.
We eat salad and talk of our passion for books.
The books are full of kisses and comings,
is this your heart in the literature
you show me? Is that you being tangible
between the words? I want to kiss you.

If you look up from your book now,
if there is a chink in your protection,
I will feed your heart with my mouth and tongue.
Kiss the words into being and us
into something more than this discussion
we've been having for weeks about how
this word sits up against this word.

Adultery

Finally I reached across the table
to touch your face, the pads of my fingers
on your forehead first, drawing down near
the inner edge of your ear and under
to hold your chin, lifting your head slightly
as if I'm about to kiss you.

We are burning as if we are adulterers.
The table is between us to keep us apart.
I think if we are going to have to pay for this,
I want to have at least touched your skin.
We do not kiss, don't go home, or make love,
we drink tea—green for you, regular black tea
for me. I eat, you say you can't.

We are adulterers of talk and desire,
pretending that by not coming together
we are somehow still standing on the good side
of the line.

We sit amongst other lovers, no one knows
we are not supposed to be, *say my name,* you say,
and I say it. *I want to show you so many things,*
you say. It goes right into the place
I have covered up and armoured, to pretend
it no longer existed.

Most of the Things That Need to be Seen are Seen with the Eyes Closed

1

It is as if I am being asked to love without
grasping. I have no idea how to love you
without desire, anyone else but not you,
for though we are not, you once described
to me the voice a poppy has for the sun,
the knowledge moss has of the meaning of
stone as it glows in alcoves of tree shade.

2

With the simplest of looks you undid the knot
of holding in me—so now I have no idea
how to do what I am being asked, not
through the holding of breath, or the waiting
through time, of journeys into the inners
with prayers of letting go. When you kissed
the unseen in me it was not the awakening
of suddenness.

3

To stop seeing all I have to do
is open my eyes and look at these sights,
these lies: red brick of a school building,
silver greys of clouds and sea, the green of
a wet English summer.

Lightly

I want to make you come with just my tongue.
I want to make you come by barely touching you.
I will start by kissing the corner of your mouth,
gently moving deeper. First one corner,
then the other. Tracing the edge of your top lip
as if I am tasting you there.
I will kiss your throat into offering.
Draw my nails up your legs. Start my finger's
journey way down at your feet, then slowly,
slowly scratch over your thighs and hips.
Over your stomach, to palm your breasts.
Settling my tongue, flicking your left nipple.
Moving your legs apart, softly entering,
just taking your pulse.
The first two fingers of my right hand
test the moisture around our connection,
then bringing your taste and smell with them.
I taste my fingers before pinching the hard peak
of your right breast, beginning to tune your dial.
Long out breath. My mouth moves
behind your ear. I put two fingers into your mouth.
Stubble grinds your cheek, and we come around to
start again at your lips. I lick the corners.
We are slowing down time for our own pleasure.
As light as we can bear it.

Green Dogs

We lay melted in green light, stretched out like dogs in their total gift of themselves. My hand on her belly, so much so that we were both completely pregnant. The light seemed to come from the child and be both of us, and we were one moment, with the gentleness of dog kisses to heal a wound. We were like that. We were one day.

Each day is anchored into that harbour; words, faces, walks, work, are turned over and over in my hands. Each surface felt and checked, each corner, any mark. Arcing back in sex magic. Life spent trying to live one day. Parcels turned over and over inside oneself looking for jewelled light.

At night we lay, not able to sleep. We slipped into space beyond sleep, where microcosmic trembling lifts like some veil. Like dogs unravelled and unified with each other. A trinity that became without expectation.

For Our Final Fuck of the Afternoon

She has me touch her where the hurt
happened over twenty years ago,

with Vaselined fingers—a gentle circle,
not entering that space but keeping
a light pressure while we move.

She is on top of me in the tipsy afternoon,
an empty champagne bottle on the table,
the plates left with the vegetables
and juices from lunch.

We both come here to heal our bodies
in the letting go, in saying yes,
finding the perceived darkness full
of light and occasional guttural tears.

There is no thing to fear in each other,
simply as man and woman. I say *keep the rhythm,*
and slow her down, she wants to speed up
to get to the cumming. *Just like that,*
hold the rhythm, the slowburn and the sobs come,
as I take the line, reach into manliness
not in command but in certainty, *roll into me.*

No depletion from this day of love and lunch
and more love. We have cut this afternoon out
of the universe to explore our shadows and lights,
then we will bathe and sleep, absorbing the life
we have taken back from the mouth of death.

Sunday

We always wake early and talk the big questions,
the tiny things. Drink tea and talk more.
The threat of having to get up
makes us make morning love.

We slip in and out of consciousness,
facing each other on our sides.
She is relaxed-faced and burring slightly.
Each breathing makes me want to kiss her skin.
The arm, the belly, behind her knees, the tops of her feet,
her cheek, her forehead. Feel the soft hair above her lip.
I am wet with her. My penis and my lower belly.
She trickles between my legs, making sticky corners
where my legs join my body.
She breathes in, breathes out.

Love Poem

I want the next thing I write to have you in it,
I always do. I want to write about your hair,
or your hands, or the smile you have when you
crack with emotion. But the next poem
has a white wall in it, and a halogen lamp
that's so bright, it leaves ghost trails in the eyes,
and is dangerously hot to touch.

The next poem has got a beech wood in too, or rather
the path that runs through the wood, and a meeting
with a dog who smiles when you greet her.
It will be a love poem, the next poem with you in.
They always are love poems, even when they turn out
to have bombs in them, or politics, or light switches.

Via Negativa

I could have loved each of you so much better
than I did. You remained sitting at my table
and sharing my bed for so long.

For so long I heard my own voice instead
of each of yours. I had not learned
to make anything, to put a brick
on top of another brick, to plant seeds
in a field, to put one word up against another.
To know a day and to name it summer.

Each of us choosing and chasing
the reflections that suited the feeling.
We could not be other than we were.

Dark trees before bud.
Hands reaching for hands.
Blood seeking blood,
voice for voice, and bodies
looking to quench themselves
without learning seawater
from freshwater.

We could have loved so much better
than we did. For so long we sat at the table
waiting, while not one of us served the other.
For so long our voices were filled with only
the words we knew. Without knowing what lay
between those words. Brick by brick, seed by seed,
body next to body, summer day by day.
Without knowing who lies behind each feeling.

The bud before blossom.
An open hand.
Knowledge of the sanguine.
Waiting for the other to speak.
We could not be other than we were.

Four Wishes:
A leaf with knowledge of the root.
Hands working with love then taking your hand
at the end of day. A moment rather than
more words. A jug of clean water on the table.

The Tree of Life

We tell ourselves stories in order to live
— JOAN DIDION

Making

When it was just me—I had no memory or breath,
I had lived alone for so long inventing prayers.
Full and empty—without possibility or change.
Glaciers moved like lightning, mountains became sand,
suns birthed and died, universes bloomed and dissipated
—all of them pinpricks against the long dark.

Let it be dark—I made the darkness.
Breaking apart the poverty of existence
        —out of endless aching boredom.
Let it be light—I will plant a garden here.
When?—I will become the grass, the trees,
the flowers and the fruit.
I could walk there—begin there. When?
I had existed without beginning.
Had not conceived that for there to be life
there has to be the absoluteness of ending.

Let it be dark—Lilith came out of a dream,
then she was next to me. Let it be light.
We made thunder and time. We made the garden
after days in bed talking. We made new words,
made ourselves, went out into the new.

I became the grass to seed in the sun,
she the rainfall weighed by the seasons.
I became the trees, she became the fruit of the world.
We learned our lessons, observing, writing, feeding.
We made twelve trees—each one part of ourselves.

We fight in the garden—oh how we fight,
even when we are not speaking we hold each other
in the night. We fight with our fire,
        —we fall into the river making steam.

One tree split as if two trees
        —I gave the bright half my knowledge,
she gave the dark half her secrets.
        The prevailing cool breeze turned its limbs.

On another tree we pinned bright things of hope,
bright things written in verses, and totems
buried at the roots. We hung streamers
and lights, which we lit at night.
Glass jars pulled from the bin, washed the labels off
        —painted the glass, red and green and orange.
Night-light rituals of becoming. We made a tree of life.

When I am you and you—me—becoming.
We are the garden: grass, trees and the fruit.

In the autumn it fruited—twelve kinds of fruit
on the one tree, we ate apples of life,
pears of hope, berries of love.

I became clean, gave her my darkness, my light,
my animal body, my memory and breath.
We spoke our names,
        spoke of marriage, the days to come.

She gave her darkness, became clean.
Gave her animal body, her soul, her light,
breath and memory. Our days, our marriage,
    our life in the garden.

This is the garden we made to know each other,
as we learned that life had to be acceptable.
I made her a platter of fruits from the trees.
I put fresh sheets on the bed for our wedding day.
I put away the spectral thought forms of the long dark.
When I am you and you — me — becoming.
We are the garden: grass, trees and the fruit.

Detail

Amongst the fleshy leaves.
Amongst the blossom
         —the potential of fruit.
The hummingbird taking nectar
from the trumpet throats of the flowers.

Unwritten

Unwrite her name. Undo the letters of
her name. Take away all reference of her
from your bibles and your scrolls, take God's wife
from him and make him in your own image.
Make him lonely; make him what you need him
to be. Make her a daemon, a screech owl,
a succubus, an invader of your unspoken dreams.

Circumnavigations
Trial One — The Root of the Root

Reclaiming my body — my soul.
In desire, in woman after woman.
Waiting for you to exist again.

Each love — the root of the root.
Each lover a shadow of my love.
Reclaiming my body, my soul.

The heat of nightly fuckings,
burning out the core of despair.
Waiting for you to exist again.

We could have loved so much better
than we did — we are all that we are.
Reclaiming my body, my soul.

That I should say your name, my name.
That I should forget your name, while
waiting for you to exist again.

Your words are in my mouth.
Your tongue animates my tongue.
You are desire — the women of my life.
I am waiting for you to exist again.

Circumnavigations
Trial Two— Ritual of the Sun

Her belly against my belly.
Silencing the guilt of seeking.
Moments of stillness and fullness.

Placing the heat of the sun where
the dark blood centres in seeking.
Her belly against my belly.

The Ritual of the Sun,
kindled by friction, dancing at dawn
in moments of stillness and fullness.

Closing the curtains, keep the fire lit.
Don't point at the sun in wickedness.
Her belly against my belly.

Naked at dawn amongst the lime trees,
quench this fire, eye of heaven. Give me
moments of stillness and fullness.

Rituals of circumnavigation,
walking the sphere and the cube,
the forest and the cities seeking
moments of stillness and fullness.

Circumnavigations
Trial Three — Action

Action is character they say.
Each person acts, each action is
character, is life with or without

meaning. The simplest thing,
a movement, a gesture, a kiss.
Action is character they say.

The right of action born from
belonging, overcoming shame.
Character is life with or without

belonging. The feel of the ground
under my shoes, each step leads me.
Action is character they say.

Putting the past away, remember
to find joy in the gestures, the kisses.
Character is life with or without

memory. The simplest things:
movements, gestures, kisses.
We act or we are acted upon.
Character is life with or without

Circumnavigations
Trial Four—Sin Eating

Bread and salt to eat the sin of sorrow.
Clean the heart and the mind and the body.
Bread and salt—to love and to be loved.

Following the sin-eaters I formed
a black house in the garden that we made.
Bread and salt to eat the sin of sorrow.

Following the forgetting of your face,
I said your name aloud over and over.
Bread and salt—to love and to be loved.

After searching for you in the depths of
each lover, I would hear your name again.
Bread and salt to eat the sin of sorrow.

After ecstasy we would count white stars,
rename the constellations marking time.
Bread and salt—to love and to be loved.

I repainted the house of the heart,
Gave up searching for love, so that I could
love and be loved—no sin, only choices.
Bread and salt—to love and to be loved.

Circumnavigations
Trial Five—A Gospel of Silence
(Pygmalionism)

Silence made from all the things we say.
The question, which makes (my body, my soul)
the one thing we most want to speak out loud is

in the town at night, in the bars,
at work, in the profound moments of love
        —silence made from all the things we say.

The weight of the tongue muted against time,
unknowing (almost knowing)
the one thing we most want to speak out loud is

constant at the root of each thought,
the root of each root, the words of the body,
the silence made from all the things we say.

A pressure within the throat, or a cold clear
night when we consider the names of stars.
The one thing we most want to speak out loud is

never said, or if it is, it is not heard,
even if we are capable of forming it in black ink
on white paper, it pulls the stars apart.
The one thing we most want to say out loud is

Circumnavigations
Trial Six—Shadows

Root to sky before the branches,
clarity comes at such a price.
Satan's along for the ride.

The unfound words and frustrated love,
the beautiful yes, the give of the fruit.
Root to sky before the branches.

The light of the morning star.
The best delusion is the thing itself.
Satan's along for the ride.

The spaces between the cells of being,
as vibrant as the light of the morning star.
Root to sky before the branches.

There is evil in this world,
makes no difference how well we see it.
Satan's along for the ride.

I always felt divided, days when I didn't know
who you were, days when I had no love for you,
days when words were as empty as justice.
Satan's along for the ride.

Circumnavigations
Trial Seven—Love and the Body

and all there is, is love and the body,
nothing to give but this moment,
and this moment and this moment.

And all there has ever been is you and I
so easily lost in the feelings, the reaching,
and all there is, is love and the body.

All these faces and you and I
the space between, like the morning light,
and this moment, and this moment.

Surrounded by your sound, as if bees
were swarming, or a distant voice calling your name,
and all there is, is love and the body.

Our bodies, our trees of life.
The fruit of ourselves, giving and self-giving,
and this moment and this moment.

You are an unanswered question.
All there is, is love and the body.
Action of blood, character, skin, muscle, thought,
and this moment and this moment.

Tree of Life

Sunshine, white and red. Small glass panes set
in white window frames turned to bonewood.

The bench in front of the house, the veranda
with its newels like old teeth—both the same.
Their wood, patient with fingerprints from hands
that have waited and forgotten how to wait.

I built the house at the edge when I met her.
Lilith is gone—our love was fiery,
we kept our promises both thick and thin,
but one always goes before the other.

I took in the dogs then, a pair of strays
from the desert. I talk with them
as I talk to myself—the way old people do
when days are filled with themselves, simple routines:
walking to the mailbox, feeding the boys.

An old man, with his white house at the edge,
his two dogs, and his routines. I made the world
with my power, created time with my hands,
my rage, my mind and my words. At night Lilith
and I made love that shook the sky with thunder.
We made the garden: as poets, life-givers.

I wait for a visit on the white veranda,
shaded by the roof in these blasting hot days.
The roof tar melted off long ago.
I took the fence down to make the garden
part of the world. The trees were for us all
to eat the fruit of. I hope the children
will stop by to pick the fruit.

Xibulba

We will walk—on the land
We will breathe—of the air
We will drink—from the stream
We will live—hold the line

— PETER GABRIEL

Lustre

Gold, silver and copper as reflection and as light.
Symbols of the dream life, the good life, as myth.

To never dim as the hands of day pass on into time.

A question for beauty, are you truth? Are you home?
Earth formed into a vase, a vessel for the spirit.

The art of beauty—I shine for you to catch your eye,
to wake your soul, with cupped hands which
close around the hands of day.

Transmute the colours of elements.
Place copper against red.
Place gold against blue.
Take fire from the wet earth.
Burn a butterfly in brightness.

The artist as alchemist, breathing soul into clay,
shaping love and beauty, learn them with your hands.
Learning how to live them, day after day.

Heat and time brings the colour,
to know beauty is to know their gift.
Place a vessel of spirit into their hands to become
undimmed against the fading
          —against the closing of the day.

Xibulba

My bed had become my coffin.
My life a cemetery of memorial stones
for pasts that I had dreamed and laid to rest.

My body ripened with decay and gasses
under soil. Nails and beard grew. My flesh
putrefied and became liquid, leaked into the earth.
My skull emptied its brains into dirt.

A seed fell in a bird's shit and my elements
fed the tree, which after years bore fruit
under sun and rain. As the memorial stones
grew mossy, the weather chipped at their names.

I came into the garden to pick fruit
from the tree. The father of myself,
I know the names of names. You come to stand
with me. We sit on my headstone and I tell you
the stories of the names on the stones,
and you tell me yours.

Around us a small brown bird speaks *tchichoo,*
tchichoo. We give thanks for this day in our lives.

Why?

Because we love it. Because we hate it. Because it
is Northern. Because it is Southern. Because this is
England. Because of the sea at our edges.
Because we live here. Because we were born here.
Because of habit. Because of the myth of returning.
Because we don't want to be here.
Because there is nowhere else. Because we came
here as a child. Because it is cheap/friendly
familiar/true/known. Because of the lights.
Because of the sex. Because of the pubs. Because
of the nights. Because you have to live somewhere.
Because of love. Because it holds our secrets.
Because this is what we know. Because people
talk to you. Because the sun manages to shine.

Full Blood

Awake on a mountain path
surrounded by butterflies.
I cannot hold or possess them.
They fly just ahead of my steps.
There is nothing to do but be here.

Gauntlets

I caught the moon and turned it into a swastika.
I caught the sun and turned its arms back to make
a swastika. Spun their cloth to make sleeves, and wore
them both as gauntlets on my arms as I walked
from Europe to India in the space of a morning,
between leaving for school and the lunch bell.

France was hanging out its washing. Germany
was peeling potatoes. Austria had decided to linger
in the bath, and Yugoslavia was choosing her dress
for the dance. Turkey was craving strong dark chocolate
when it should have been working.
Iraq was brewing up tea. Iran was asking Afghanistan
to marry him, and she was taking her time.

Note: There are two types of swastika used in Indian symbolism:
The Sun Swastika—drawing on the day and the light as a symbol of good
luck.
The Moon Swastika—drawing on the night and the subconscious as a symbol
of deeper feelings and desires.

We Will Wake at Dawn

Waiting beyond suffering,
our lives are entangled.

There are snakes.
There are hours filled
with dreams of march hares
with black tipped ears.

I wait for you to come,
heart-bruised and naked,
carrying a price that I will
take on my own head.

In dreams we are new.
The wild moon lighting
the blown-away sky
with a halo.

The wild moon lighting
dark high fields above the town.

Between your breasts—a kiss
to penetrate, to love, the torn places
you made in your leaving for home.

I give you water, eggs, oranges, toast.
I give you my arms and chest, my root.

You are dying to be born anew,
to become a bride with her dress
blowing around her, as we stand
together on the hilltops entangled
like tree branches grown close.
How wild the moon.

We will wake at dawn,
married, beside each other,
as if we have always been.

Mary

She headed west
twenty years ago,
got to the edge,
stopped. Today
she is smoking
a cigar in a holder.
It is a fine cigar,
smoke clouds around.
It is deep as she
rolls it on
her palate letting it rise
naturally from her.
It tastes good to her.

Blackpool Rock

One new year's eve
we drove out of the city,
brought candles, incense
and wishes for love
—an assembled family

of siblings and lovers.
We parked up at Bispham,
took our shelter by the sea wall,
to light our lights. We said
our wishes in rhythm
with the crashing of the sea
against the defenses.

While the drinkers drink.
While Auld Lang Syne sounds out.
While the black sky covers us.
While the sea crash speaks
to the spray and plume in each of us.
Resolutions made
      in Bispham Shelters.
The lights of Blackpool
      twinkling to the south.

Rain Song

On the third day of the British rainy season,
in a café fogged by breath, coffee steam, moisture
from fried breakfasts. The relief of getting
them off to school, the quick stop before knuckling
down to the day. The rain turns on,
words like bucketing and pouring,
words like downpour and monsoon.

The sound comes up, and everyone stops,
stops eating, stops talking, all eyes turn
to the grey fogged window, all eyes begin
slow smiles. We nestle into the rain-song
as if it were a duvet and we're hiding
upstairs, a game with our mum and dad.
No one will be the first to speak,
to give the game away.

How to Sleep

Take pear juice
and blend it with soma
to make an embryo,
who will grow through the rains
to become a copper-coloured man,

who will leave his ten white horses
grazing while he kisses you on the forehead,
leaving you clear as the sieve of the sky,
as blue crystal.

How to Become a Moth

Constantly defy expectation
until one night you are
airborne.

Night is long and life is short,
soak in moonlight,
avoid flames.

A lover will call to you by scent
across a mile or two,
measured by the scales of wings.

Feed from the UV glowing flowers
guiding your tongue deep
to the nectar.

On Becoming a Writer

Learn to sit and be invisible,
surround yourself with ordinary
things. Take no notes in public.

A glass of water with your coffee
will let you sit for longer.
Never appear interested in the talk.

Be plain on the outside. Inside
your mouth is a diamond; never
speak of it before you set its ways in ink.

Bailero

I wake up pregnant and piss like a horse
in a pre-dawn field, with the ragwort still
asleep, and fences surrounding
the wetness of mystery.

Back curved, all ears, the sound of no sound.
Across the valley floor there might be singing.
I hold my breathing. Is it singing?
'I will carry you across the water.'

Rub my legs as if I am my own lover.
The tightness of shins under downward fingers.
The sky under a pale of yellow.
The grass is lively under my feet.

The Road

Carrying my father home.
His photograph pressed between the pages
of a notebook as if he were some flower
cut and kept for the memory, but as
with all memories locked into pages
and books, unless someone records the details,
the name, the place, a record of the event,
then things get lost to the linearity of time.

I am to carry my father.
I am my father's son.
I am my father's father.
I carry him in my cells,
in my pages, in my mouth,
in every word I do not say.
He is the absence of silence.
The solitude of noise.
He is the road that leads out
of the city to the country.
I am the one who takes
the road both directions.

Become

India is my father.
Stop doubting who you are.

Jullundur is my shrine,
I say prayers to my ancestors here.

India is my wife, with her
I lay down my burdens.
Become a man again.
I take her strongly in my arms.
We are man and woman together.
I am the earth and she is the sky.

Eagle

In the greens of a backstreet park,
where winter sun is as warm as
British summertime, an eagle
takes flight for me, through the trees
and over the town. A travelling eye
for a man who doesn't know where to go.

A straight course over the unplanned
confusion of Jullundur's streets
which have fallen in love with cars,
so that they have forgotten
to put any pavement down.

I fly over flat white roofs.
Watch a priest ring his bell,
beat the bounds,
bless the square and the houses,
in his orange clothes
and feathered headdress.

Away with the bird, over the car horns,
past darba salesmen, and the pleading
right hands of bright-eyed beggar children.

I need not go anywhere,
the bird will travel for me.
My own body is wing, feather and eye.
I am Punjabi winter sun reflecting off the green.
The thermal rise over heavy traffic.

God speaks not in words today,
but in the flesh of the bird,
a glint of light.

Carry your father,
                    become your own mother.
You are your own country,
                    father of your father.
Give birth to wing, feather,
                    poem, eye and sun.

Love Poem
(for A.G.)

I will take you strongly in my arms,
sky over my earth.

I will leave my burdens down,
earth over my core.

I will love you as
the sun lights a bird's back.

I will stand with you as
we give our hearts to life's great keeping.

Sky over my earth.
Lay your burdens down.
Earth over molten core.
Sun on a bird's back.

Keeping our promise to live by living.

I will take you strongly in my arms.

Jali

Returning from the sun to return to his son.
Bouncing harp notes from the plate glass
of Superdrug.

Cutting the air with proud chin,
with cigarette smoke, with music passed
from his father's hands into his fingers.
Returning from Gambia to return to his son.

The kora is life. Life in Piccadilly Gardens
made clean and crystal, lifted spirit,
as we approach and leave.
Intersections of buses and trams;
Altrincham one way, Bury the other.
Cross-cutting the notes of time and pitch
to hold his life together.

Humanity is different here, he says.
People don't know about each other.
Music penetrates us with imported humanity.
I don't play for money, I play for our souls.

There are bargains to be had in Superdrug,
two deodorants for the price of one.
Away down Market Street there are other musics,
the loop of a Romanian waltz played on accordion,
a French tango by the escalators near the shoe shops.

If you come here before the music starts,
you have to imagine the life of the city.
Jali with his kora, his amp and car battery
for power, riding in on the silver tram
as the shoppers gather. Chiming in the cold sun,
in the landscaped square where we pass by,
leaving our trails as music on the air.

Kitying

Becomes Crystal
        —changing state at the age of twelve.

Makes a new name with her left hand,
cutting the facets of each letter with intention.

Polishing smooth each cut to gleam in the light.
Puts her foot forward
        —changing state, when standing still.

She has made herself, made herself, made herself
become Crystal
        —Kitying from Hong Kong.

Helps her mother with the left hand of duty and love.
Gets lost watching Eastenders, letting go of all the making.

Stands in two worlds with two names.
Pausing for breath when the money runs out.

Changing state:
Looking at the sky as the starlings flock and swoop.
To be only flight, the transparency of movement.

Changing state:
Compressing feathers to carbon, carbon to Crystal.

Clear as the light first thing in the morning.
Still and always in flight, she is making herself.

Abha

The Earth loves the first ray of light that falls
upon him each morning more than any other light.

She is the first ray, the only one.
Day has its beauty but nothing pleases the Earth
more than the first moment when Abha takes his hand.

What a risk to take for love?
Five thousand miles and a failing marriage,
a cat's cradle of ties holding her there.

Moving with the sunlight as it tracks his face
he is the world under her; without each other
there is only darkness and bare rock.

What did the Earth know before
the first ray of light of the morning?
That darkness was all and forever.
His hardness, the absence of life.
A cold dream of a star.
The meaning of being untouched.

What did the light know before
she reached out to take Earth's hand?
Pure speed through endless darkness.
No reflection of herself in the mirror.
A cold dream of a distant Earth.
The meaning of not touching.

From Chandigarh to Manchester
for a man she only knows by heart
        —the imagined city of love.
Imagine a city without light,
or the light without a city.
How small the world of the heart?

The world has conurbated,
it's a small world they say.
How large the world is
when travelled for love,
when we count the hours
and the miles lived without it.

Maria

One. Two. Three.
When she got up that morning, she looked in
on the children still in their beds. She went
downstairs and made sweet tea.

Holding hands in a line as they walk,
no looking back at the family house
they can't afford anymore.

A wren on a gatepost pays them no heed.
Her eyes fill with tears. The wren flies away.

A train across Europe, counting long hours.
Trees zip past. A ferry. Another train.
An address on a piece of paper.
Not imagining the city or the next day.
She hums a waltz to the children,
one, two, three.

Two. Two. Three.
Black scarf to keep her warm,
accordion on her chest.
An empty waltz for shoppers,
you can almost sing along.

Back before she left him
they would have danced to this
on Friday nights, counting time
in Bucharest, in the dim lights
of the dance hall, a round of drinks
waiting at their table.
Endless night of footsteps
counting the time of their marriage,
two, two, three.

Three. Two. Three.
Harp music from up towards Piccadilly.
The blast of sound from HMV.
Always the same position against the pillar,
British Home Stores. This is the waltz
of a woman who has made herself invisible
by the lowering of her eyes.

Her children teach her English
though she never likes to speak it.
The same few notes every day.
The same faces of the shoppers everyday.
The same looks. The same empty waltz.
There is a woman on Market Street who
is not there. She is waiting without waiting,
counting out time, three, two, three.

Junmo

Hibiscus petals falling—South Korea
puts her son on a plane for East Sussex,
you are the generations of family moving forward,
a strong brown river. Junmo's mouth is numb.

All around the boy is the rabble
of boarding school noise, they are the young
of wealthy aspiration, inheritors of the earth.

He is three months silent.
His numbness is extreme and perfect.
As they try to speak to him the pine tree
on the mountain stands unchanged.

At night he is a soldier, by the light
of his computer screen.
Lieutenant Jimmy Patterson moving
behind enemy lines. Thumbs moving
his mind through intrigue and heroics.

Language melts as wind and frost are blown away,
Roses of Sharon bloom as he moves
to northern quarters. Arms folded to keep his heart in.
A piecemeal plan:
sell hats,
make money,
buy a three bedroom house.

Around him is the random noise of shoppers,
students, goths and new emos with their mums.
How will he inherit the earth?

In the end it's his breeding,
a simple act of belief passed on,
a seed to a flower, the simplest thing.

He would like someone to speak to him,
though he can't quite meet someone's eyes.
Saturday is the busiest day,
selling hats and leather bound journals.
At night he is a soldier, his thumbs on the controller.

Note: This poem draws its shape and imagery from Ezra Pound's 'The Garden,' and The South Korean National Anthem.

Flowing

She stands in the late morning light holding
her robe open. My spunk running down her legs,
like three large drops leaving trails of first rain
on a window in early spring.

We had made love for the first time in days,
you know how life sometimes gets in the way
of the things you need.

We made love gently, nothing wild, just togetherness.
Our brown skins
      —my coarseness against her smooth.

She loves me coming inside her,
it makes me complete she says.
I need nothing other than to keep
looking into her eyes, seeing her face
close to mine, an all over touch.

Sometimes we get real crazy,
but this morning was meant to be
nothing more than a late morning kiss.
Getting caught up in it
      —something deeper,
a closeness, a need for union.

Now she brazenly stands just after
with her white bathrobe open,
her cunt still swollen,
something of me flowing down her legs.

Sky Burial

The coldest morning,
white and blue.
Dazzling windows,
brilliant and pale,
colourless and yet full.

Empty the sky.
Empty the streets.
The Blackening
—vision out and in.

Iron trees—perfectly
sculptural,
dense as the earth
—rain, fire, sap, wood.
Without a throat
or a song.
Full of song.

A crow held by
the light, upswirl,
contrast and question,
lustre of feathers.

Contrast and question.
Bird against sky.
Light without heat.
Light exploded
in the darkness.
No break between
the moments
of before and after.

Pulled apart,
fed to the birds.
All that I am is divisible.

All that I am
is the question of
a crow against the sky
on a cold morning
when it is too bright
to see,
too blue and white
to believe.
The tree against
the landscape. One thing
depending on the other.

A Place of Silence

You stand high on the rocks
overlooking the lake.
I lie near you recalling my life,
how I had waited for you before
I knew you. How I had waited
in a place made of my own silence.
It was a room filled with tables,
couches and other lovers.
It was a house where everything
was perfect. It was a tree where
I tied my prayers up with red ribbons.

You stand high on the rocks looking
down at the water. I lie back on the rock,
straightening my spine. Warm exposed
skeleton of the earth in the sunshine.

Love is a verb.
To love you is to serve God.
Each day presents itself.

In this place of silence the clouds
scud across the sky driven by high winds.
We are the children of the earth.
We are woman and man and earth and God.
This is how we begin

Further Acknowledgements

Thanks are due to many people who have inspired the contents of this book, however special mention must be made to:

Catherine Smith, without her wonderful editing eye & her belief in my work there would be no books.
The team at Salt, who give me free rein to write the books I want to write.
Fundacion Valparaiso, Mojacar, Spain, for space and time to create.
The British Council, for providing me with a poetry residency in Los Angeles, which led to a number of the works in this volume.
California State University, Los Angeles for being such a kind host.
Blackpool Libraries and Arts for time, funding and belief in the work.
Kriyta Poetry Festival, India for inviting me to read, and providing the mechanisms to explore and create a number of the poems in this volume.
Nek Chand for graciously receiving this wandering poet into his beautiful sculpture garden at Chandigarh.
The Department of Transcultural Writing at Lancaster University for commissioning the poems: 'Jali', 'Kitying', 'Abha', 'Maria', and 'Junmo'.
The Ministry Of Defence for information, which aided 'One Hundred (Part One).'
Professor Marc Herold for information, which aided 'One Hundred (Part Two).'
'Every Atom' commissioned through Alchemy by Bradford

Culture, Tourism & Sport and iMove. Inspired by London 2012. iMove is funded by The Legacy Trust UK, Yorkshire Forward & Arts Council England. Thanks to Northern School of Contemporary Dance who used this poem as the basis for a series of performances.

'Why' and 'Blackpool Rock' were commissioned by Blackpool Libraries and Arts, and Blackpool Council.

'Thirst' was commissioned by Alchemy for The Cultural Leadership Initiative.

'Lustre' and 'True Roses of England' were commissioned by Manchester Literature Festival & Manchester Art Gallery as part of a longer series of poems based on the exhibition 'Exporting Beauty'.

Xibulba epigraph—extract from San Jacinto (Peter Gabriel) Reprinted by permission.
Published by Real World Music Ltd.
International Copyright secured.
Courtesy of petergabriel.com

A LIST:
Abha Gautam, Adonis, Kath and Ann Siddique, Xanthe Gresham, Stephen Hughes, John Holland, Danielle Colclough, Sue Hartley, Claire Chambers, Chris Hamilton-Emery, Cherry Smyth, Nima Poovaya-Smith, Peter Kalu, Roberto Cantu, Walter Santucci, Katie Chatburn, Beth Cuenco, Jane May, Greg Klerx, Marina Benjamin, Jackie Kay, Peter Gabriel, Bella Lacey, Emily Greenhouse and Ollie Brock at GRANTA Magazine, Fiona Sampson at Poetry Review. Mike Mackmin at The Rialto.

Lightning Source UK Ltd.
Milton Keynes UK
UKOW05f1326250813

215930UK00002B/17/P